MW01243251

AFRIKAANS CHILDREN'S BOOK

Alice in Wonderland
(English and Afrikaans Edition)

WAI CHEUNG

This page intentionally left blank.

ABOUT THE BOOK

Raise your children in a bilingual fashion with this bilingual coloring book that captures the magic and beauty of Alice in Wonderland's story along with a dual language storytelling that is perfect for parents who want to raise their children in a bilingual environment.

CONTENTS

This page intentionally left blank.

Alice saw the White Rabbit pause for a moment to check the time on his pocket-watch.

Alice het die Wit Haas gesien 'n breek neem vir 'n oomblik om na die tyd op sy sak-horlosie te kyk.

3

Plate 1.
Rabbit

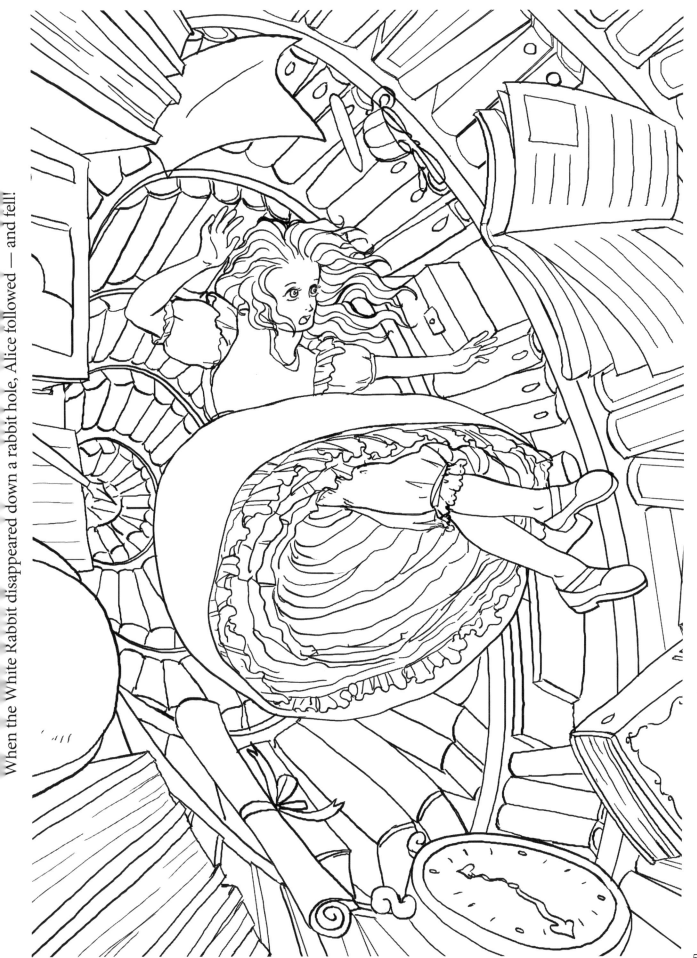

When the White Rabbit disappeared down a rabbit hole, Alice followed — and fell!

Wanneer die Wit Haas af 'n haas gat verdwyn het, het Alice gevolg - en het geval!

Plate 2.
Falling

Alice finally stopped falling, so she began to walk and encountered the Caterpillar.

Alice uiteindelik tot stilstand geval so sy het begin om te loop en toe die Caterpillar ontmoet.

Plate 3.
The Caterpillar

She next met and looked up at the large grin of the Cheshire Cat.

Sy het volgende ontmoet en na die groot glimlag van die Cheshire Kat opgekyk.

Plate 4.
Cheshire Cat

Alice had tea with the very mad March Hare and Hatter, as well as the sleepy Dormouse.

Alice het tee met die baie mal Maart Hare en Hatter gehad sowel as die vaak Dormouse.

Plate 5.
Tea Party

After the tiring tea party Alice saw three playing cards standing under a rose bush, ready to paint the white roses red.

Na die uitputtend teeparty het Alice drie speelkaarte sien staan onder 'n roosboom, gereed om die wit rose rooi te verf.

13

Plate 6.
Painting Roses

Alice soon met the Queen of Hearts, who was quick to yell, "Off with her head!"

Alice het binnekort die Koningin van Harte ontmoet, wat vinnig was om te gil, "Af met haar kop!"

15

Plate 7.
The Queen

All the madness that lie at the bottom of the rabbit hole swirled around Alice in a dream-like whirlwind...

Al die waansin wat aan die onderkant van die haas gat lê het rondom Alice gekrul in 'n droom-agtige warrelwind...

Plate 8.
The Cards

18

ABOUT THE BOOK

Raise your children in a bilingual fashion with this bilingual coloring book that captures the magic and beauty of Alice in Wonderland's story along with a dual language storytelling that is perfect for parents who want to raise their children in a bilingual environment.

This page intentionally left blank.